CX LEAIN

Healthy Lifestyles

BALANCING WORK & PLAY

Camilla de la Bédoyère

Contents

Introduction 6

Managing Your Life 8

Making the Most of You 12

Time for Work 18

Choices and Changes 24

Under Pressure 28

The Best You Can Be 32

Friends and Family 38

A Bright Future 42

Glossary 44

Further Information 45

Index 46

Introduction

You are the sum of all your parts. This means that the genes you got from your parents, the environment in which you live and the experiences you have had, have all contributed to this perfect blend of a person – you.

Who are you?

As a child, adults made most of the big decisions about what would happen to you. As you move towards adulthood, however, you begin to share in the responsibility for those decisions. This can be a tricky time, because there are so many things going on around you, and so many people to please – including family, teachers and friends. The challenge you face is to carve yourself a clear path through the maze of work and play, obligations and distractions. Choosing to manage your life puts you in charge.

A perfect balance

If you were asked to list the activities you need to do, or like to do, they would probably fall into two main groups: work and play.

Work includes school studies, paid employment and chores or responsibilities you have around the home. Work is something you may sometimes enjoy doing, but it's also likely to be something you *have* to do. Work usually offers important benefits – such as earning money, new skills and improved career opportunities.

DiD YOU KNOW?

According to young people themselves, three of the most important – and stressful – issues they need to deal with are exams, bullying and family break-ups.

Play includes hobbies, socialising, sport or just relaxing at home. Play is probably something you want to do, but it is just as important to your well-being as work, allowing you to exercise and enjoy new experiences.

Equilibrium means balance. When you have equilibrium in your life it means you have the perfect balance between work and play. This balance can be hard to achieve, but we are getting better at understanding how important it is to find time to organise our lives, to get the most from our precious time, and keep both our bodies and minds in good health.

100 per cent yourself

You may have heard people talking about 'holistic healing'. This is an approach to health based on the belief that all parts of the human body are interconnected, and work best when they pull together. To keep yourself well you need to look after both your mental and physical health. One way to keep stress to a minimum is by trying to achieve a balance in everything you do.

Working hard is important, but so is making time for relaxation and leisure activities.

Managing Your Life

Lying beneath a protective layer of bone is possibly one of the most complex structures that the universe has ever known – your brain.

The parietal lobe is concerned with speech and information-processing.

The frontal lobe is concerned with planning, reasoning, emotions and problem-solving.

The occipital lobe is concerned with aspects of vision.

The temporal lobe is concerned with perception, recognition of sounds and memory.

The cerebellum is concerned with movement, balance and muscle tone.

The brain stem controls breathing, digestion and heart rate.

Mind over matter

Your brain is nothing special to look at, and it has a texture like warm jelly, but this incredible organ contains more than 100 billion brain cells. It can process millions of bits of information every day – and contains all your personality, memories, ideas and thoughts. The main part of the brain is called the cerebrum. Its outer, wrinkled layer is made up of millions of brain cells (neurons) and is called the grey matter. This is where most of your thinking and higher-level brain activities take place.

DiD YOU KNOW?

Your brain is responsible for only about 2.5 per cent of your body weight – a tiny amount given the many important jobs it has to do. However, it uses up about 20 per cent of your energy!

A lot of nerve

A brain cell, or neuron, has two main parts: an axon and the cell body. The axon is a long nerve fibre, which comes from the cell body and carries nerve impulses along it. Each cell body can have thousands of tiny projections, or dendrites, coming from it, which connect with other neurons. Neurons send messages to one another along the axons at speeds of up to 400 km/h. The messages can cross a tiny gap – called a synapse – from an axon to a neighbouring dendrite, building up an enormously complex web of connections.

Every time you do something, learn something or think a single thought, neurons connect with one another. It is an extraordinary process that gives you almost unlimited learning potential. There are more potential links between your brain cells than there are atoms in the whole universe.

Use it or lose it

Scientists used to believe that neurons only grew in the brains of infants. Now, with the help of new technology such as functional Magnetic Resonance Imaging (fMRI), they have learnt that neurons grow throughout life in response to learning.

Experts have also found that teenagers' brains are rather like a building site; there is an explosion of growth and change during puberty. This means that the way you use your brain now will have an enormous impact on how it develops into adulthood. For example, recent research has shown that grey matter grows greatly in young people just before puberty sets in. During puberty, the unused neurons are trimmed away and lost. Does that mean that teens get more stupid? No, it means the opposite – that teens have an incredible ability to learn.

Why? Because the experiences that you have at this stage of your life have the ability permanently alter the way your brain works. Learn how to play an instrument now, or learn a new language, and you are creating millions of new neuron connections that will become a permanent fixture in your brain. On the other hand, if you don't attempt to learn new things, or you drink alcohol at too young an age, you may lose some of your brain's incredible power – for ever. Misuse of some drugs can also have lasting effects on your brain's development.

Research has shown that during puberty you are more receptive to learning than you are as an adult.

FEEL-GOOD FACTOR

Eating omega oils may help your brain develop. These essential oils, such as omega-3 and omega-6, contain lots of DHA, a substance that helps messages zap between brain cells at top speeds. You can get omega oils from oily fish, such as salmon and mackerel, or some vegetable oils, such as flaxseed and sunflower oils.

Building brain power

Now you know what an incredible organ your brain is, the next thing to discover is how to boost its power so you can reach top performance levels. Eating well and exercising will obviously help, but making the most of the time you spend learning in school or studying at home will prove to be very rewarding. Become an effective student, who can learn the most in the shortest amount of time, and you will have more opportunities to pursue other interests. In short, it will help you achieve balance in your life.

Learn to learn

Teachers agree that there are three different learning styles, and that most of us have brains that are suited to one or two of them:

- **Kinaesthetic:** kinaesthetic learners need to do, or feel, things to learn and especially like using their hands.
- **Visual:** this method of learning suits people who like to see pictures, maps etc.
- **Auditory:** this applies to people who learn best by listening and talking.

MYELINATION

The neurons in a teen's brain undergo a process called myelination. During this process you are better at learning and adapting to new situations, but less likely to control impulses or organise yourself. This process ends in adulthood, when learning and adapting become harder.

Kinaesthetic people learn better when they can use their hands.

You may have noticed that teachers attempt to use a range of learning materials and methods that appeal to all these styles. Try to identify which learning method suits you best. For example, if you are a visual learner then taking notes in the form of mind maps may suit you. Kinaesthetic learners may find that learning French vocabulary is easier if they practise it while bouncing on a trampoline, or walking around the room. Auditory learners could record key facts on their MP3 players, and listen to them on journeys. The trick is to play to your strengths. There are plenty of websites that enable you to test the best way for you to learn. Search for 'test your learning style'.

People with visual brains learn better when they picture information as images or mind maps.

Lying down when studying is not good posture. Sit at a desk and keep the computer screen at eye level.

Are you sitting comfortably?

The way you hold your body is called posture – and a bad posture can lead to back and neck problems. When standing and walking, hold yourself straight with your shoulders back. When writing, reading or gaming, make sure your workstation is set up so that you are sitting comfortably and have enough light.

- If you use a laptop, get a stand so the screen is higher and you don't have to stoop to see it.

- Using a separate keyboard and mouse may reduce shoulder and wrist aches.
- Relax your eyes every 15 minutes or so by looking into the distance and refocusing there.
- Get up and move every 20 to 30 minutes. Stretch your arms, rotate your shoulders and slowly move your head from side to side.
- Avoid junk food, such as sweets or crisps, while you work. Nuts and seeds make healthier snacks and boost your brain power.

REAL LIFE

'I can't tell you how much I hate coursework. But exams – they're okay. When the pressure starts, it's like a switch turns on in my brain. Suddenly, I remember stuff and my thinking becomes very sharp.' David (16)

DiD YOU KNOW?

Neuroscientists have found that you are more likely to solve a tricky problem by taking your mind off it. That allows your brain to explore new connections – and therefore find new solutions.

Making the Most of You

Now you understand how much you can achieve, it's time to work out how to manage your time, get a better night's sleep and work your body for good health.

It's okay to spend time with your friends and enjoy extracurricular activities, but remember to set aside time for work.

FEEL-GOOD FACTOR

Write a list of the important things you need to do, putting the most urgent near the top. Tick them off as you complete each one. It's a simple but rewarding way of getting things done. Keep the list somewhere everyone can see it – like on the fridge – and the adults in your life will be impressed by your organisational skills!

Manage your time

So much to do, so little time. It's a common problem we all have to deal with. One day you may have to run a home, look after your own kids and hold down a job – all at the same time. Discovering the skills to manage your time now will help you throughout your life.

1. *Prioritise. This means working out what are the most important things to do, and putting them first. School studies are probably going to be at the top of your list.*

2. *Focus. Once you have discovered which extracurricular activities you like best, be prepared to focus on just one or two of them.*

3. *Organise. Keep a diary and try to plan ahead to avoid those last-minute panics. Get school bags and sports kits ready the night before.*

4. *Say no. If you simply have too much to do then you will have to start turning down some opportunities or activities.*

5. *Ask for help. If you're finding it hard to keep on top of things, ask for help. Avoid a crisis by anticipating problems, and asking parents, carers or teachers for advice or support.*

Dealing with distractions

It can be tough to settle down to study when there are so many distractions. Most young people like to combine a bit of homework with quite a lot of instant messaging, chatting on the phone, updating profiles on social-networking sites and checking emails. While it may be true that you can multi-task and can focus on all these things at once, try to be honest with yourself. It is most likely that you will be able to work best if you concentrate on your studies but allow yourself regular breaks – every 30 minutes or so – to catch up on those other pastimes.

COUCH POTATOES

Recent research has shown that teenagers with TVs in their rooms are more likely to eat junk food, do less homework and less exercise, and are less likely to join in with family meals. They watch an average of five hours more TV every week than other teenagers.

In a virtual world

Gaming can be great fun, and getting totally immersed in a game is half the thrill, but do you make time for more active or sociable activities? Of course, it's a question of balance.

Why not keep a weekly record of the time you spend on video gaming and watching TV? You may be surprised by just how much of your life you devote to these hobbies. If you start gaming to avoid getting down to the more urgent tasks, like homework, then you may need to remind yourself of your priorities.

Don't get distracted! Spend time on your work, then make that call to your friend.

Making the Most of You

Body basics

Doctors recommend that teenagers spend at least one hour a day on physical activity, seven days a week. It doesn't sound like much, but when many young people now typically spend up to six hours a day on media such as TV, surfing the Internet and listening to music, it's easy to see why fitness levels are falling.

There are many benefits to exercising. It improves confidence and self-esteem, builds strong bones and muscles, increases fitness, provides an opportunity to meet new people and – perhaps most importantly – have fun! If organised team sports don't appeal to you, try and find another way to get active – there are plenty of options, from walking to school to yoga classes, skateboarding and dance.

There are plenty of ways to keep your body healthy through exercise. Challenge a friend to a game of tennis, or just go for a gentle jog.

Dump the junk

You know you shouldn't head for fast food when time is short, but when you only have half an hour between school and football practice, or between your part-time job and going to a film, what can you do? We all face this problem, but it's especially hard for young adults. You are still growing – boys packing on muscle and girls laying down healthy layers of fat – so your stomach screams hunger at you. These tips may help:

- Be prepared. Keep an emergency supply of fruit, nuts, high-grain energy bars and smoothies with you.
- Eat well three times a day. Make sure every meal is balanced with a range of filling foods that are low in sugar and fat but high in fibre, and fruit and vegetables.
- Skip fizzy drinks and sweets – they give you an instant sugar-high but you will feel 10 times worse once your body has finished processing these nutritionally light snacks.

Party food

Taking time out from work to get creative in the kitchen can be very fruitful. Preparing food for your family or friends is a hands-on, fulfilling hobby that enables you to experiment with ingredients and flavours.

Think of cooking as a way to relax, rather than a chore, and you will soon discover that the real joy of food doesn't come from the taste sensation; it is the delight of creating and sharing a meal. Local libraries and bookshops stock cookery books that are ideal for beginners, or you could search for recipes on the Internet.

Vitamins for vitality

If you eat a balanced diet you do not need to take supplements. Here are some of the most vital vitamins for good health:

- Vitamin A is great for the skin and eyes. It is found in eggs, fruit and vegetables.
- B vitamins are needed for energy and growth. You'll get them from certain breakfast cereals and wholefoods.
- Vitamin C fights infections. It is found in fruit and vegetables.
- Vitamin D is essential for bones and teeth. You'll get this in oily fish, dairy food and eggs. It is also absorbed by the body from sunlight.

ANAEMIA

Iron is necessary to transport oxygen around the body. A shortage of iron is called anaemia, and it can affect girls once they begin to menstruate (have their monthly periods). Symptoms include tiredness, feeling faint or breathless and looking pale. Iron-rich foods include red meat, eggs, green leafy vegetables and some breakfast cereals.

Get involved in the cooking! Learning to prepare healthy meals will have long-term benefits as you get older.

Making the Most of You

What's so special about sleep?

Sleep is essential for good health. You need it to think clearly, learn and make memories. Cut back on your shut-eye and you are more likely to have accidents, get depressed and develop heart disease. During sleep, your body releases a growth hormone – which is especially crucial for teens – and chemicals that fight infections.

Are you getting enough sleep?

Would you be shocked to discover that you should be getting between nine and 10 hours of sleep every night? That means going to bed no later than 9.00 p.m., so you can fall asleep by 9.30 p.m. – and jump out of bed bright-eyed and bushy-tailed at 7.00 a.m.!

Sleep doctors are increasingly concerned about the quality of teens' sleep, because few teens, or their carers, realise how important sleep is. In fact, doctors recommend that people going through puberty should sleep longer and deeper than others. This will give your brain and body a chance to rest and recover from the enormous growth spurt you are going through.

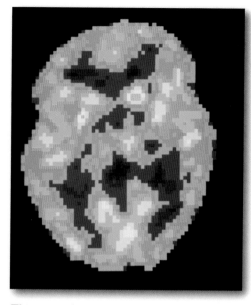

This special coloured image shows a brain that has been deprived of sleep. The red areas are the active parts of the brain and the blue are inactive. If you don't get enough sleep, your brain cannot function efficiently.

A good night's sleep is also important in tackling obesity, since sleep-deprived people crave more sweet and starchy foods. Too much sleep, however, quickly disrupts natural sleep patterns and can cause insomnia – a difficulty in falling asleep.

What controls sleep?

The pineal gland is inside the brain. It releases a hormone, melatonin, that controls sleep. The pineal gland itself is a slave to your body clock. That means your sleep patterns are affected by the amount of daylight there is. Messing with your body clock, by going to bed and getting up at different times, can upset the natural levels of melatonin, making it harder to get to sleep.

Other things affect your sleep, too: stimulants, such as caffeine in tea and coffee, block the effects of sleep hormones. Alcohol is a sedative, which means that it can help you fall asleep more quickly. However, it also disrupts the second half of your night's sleep, causing you to wake up, and disturbing your dreams. Drinking alcohol regularly can lead to sleep deprivation.

SLEEP DEPRIVATION

Most teenagers suffer from sleep deprivation. Melatonin is produced later in the evening in teens, which is why you tend to go to bed later. But you need more sleep than adults and still have to get up for school. Result? Tiredness.

Top tips for catching some zzzzz

1. *Avoid tea and coffee in the evening, and don't eat just before bedtime.*
2. *Create a routine; doing the same things every evening before bed helps settle your mind.*
3. *Exercise every day.*
4. *Avoid TV, music or other distractions in the hour before bed as they stimulate your brain, keeping you awake.*
5. *If worry is stopping you from sleeping, address the problem (see page 30).*

Age	Sleep required (hours)
6 months	12
10 years	8
15 years	9.5
Adult	8

FEEL-GOOD FACTOR

Recent research has shown that radio waves, generated by your mobile phone when you talk into it, can have the same effect as drinking a double espresso, and may delay sleep by up to 30 minutes. So, if you have problems getting to sleep you would be wise to put your phone away!

Avoid watching television in the hour before bed – it stimulates the brain and makes it harder to sleep.

Time for Work

We all have to work. Right now you have school studies and exams, but young adults are also often expected to have some paid employment. Juggling work while still finding time to play is a key life skill.

Testing times

Examinations have been used for centuries to test the knowledge and skills that people have accumulated. In fact, the remains of a diploma recorded on bronze sheets have been found dating from the Roman Empire. It proved that in AD 98 a soldier had acquired key soldiering skills! Tests are a fact of life for most students. The best way to deal with them is to follow a few simple rules.

1. Be prepared. Make sure you know when and where your exams are scheduled, and what you need to have learned for each one.

2. Keep your life in balance. Rest and relaxation, good diet and exercise are important at exam time.

3. Stay motivated. Remind yourself why these exams matter, where success can take you – and the potential consequences of a poor performance.

4. Work. You simply have to put in the hours.

Preparing for success

A revision timetable is an essential tool in preparing for exams. Sticking to it is pretty important too! If you start your revision too early you may get bored, but if you leave it too late you could feel overwhelmed by the workload. Calculate how many subjects you need to prepare for, and divide your study time between them accordingly. Organise your revision into 30-minute slots, and allow yourself time for breaks.

Studying with friends can help keep you motivated.

STRESS

Surprisingly, it is the most able students who tend to suffer the worst effects of pressure during exams. They are more likely to resort to poor techniques – such as guesswork – when they feel stressed than their less-able colleagues.

Following a revision timetable, studying hard but still taking breaks to rest and revive yourself will lead to exam success.

Put in other activities, such as sport, paid work and chores, to ensure you have a balance.

Revision is most effective when you are actively doing something; just reading your notes is not as good as reading sections and rewriting key facts, using bright colours to highlight words or concepts. Mind maps are also a great revision aid; they have been proved to significantly improve learning and memory (see page 10).

Revisiting your revision regularly strengthens neural connections, so experts recommend that you revise and make key notes to begin with, then revisit those notes 24 hours, seven days and one month later. This is sometimes called 'cascade revision', and will trigger and strengthen your neural connections.

Setting goals

Staying motivated can be hard during the lead-up to exams. Make the whole process a little more enjoyable by setting yourself goals and rewarding yourself for meeting them. For example, Adam is 14 and found it hard to start revising geography because he disliked the subject. He learnt to break up each subject into small sections – such as 'weather', 'ecosystems' and 'plate tectonics'. He rewarded himself with a bike ride, or 30 minutes of gaming, after he'd revised each one.

FEEL-GOOD FACTOR

Keeping up your healthy lifestyle during periods of revision and examinations will help your learning and performance. If you get dehydrated you may get tired and listless, and find it hard to concentrate.

Time for Work

The world of work

Working outside the home has many advantages. It gives you an income (money), experience and key skills. Many universities and colleges prefer students who have shown themselves to be motivated and responsible enough to hold down a job.

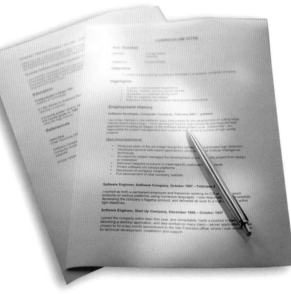

Preparing a good CV is the first step towards getting a job.

Jobs can also help you identify possible career paths.

On the downside, jobs will cut into your free time. They can also be tedious, tiring and difficult. Sometimes they involve working late, which can reduce your ability to study. It is important to find a job where the pros outweigh the cons. If work is affecting your studies, consider finding another way to earn money, and discuss the situation with your parents or carers.

Finding a job

Identify the places you would like to work, and visit them with a copy of your CV, making sure you look clean and smart. A CV lists your contact details and any work experience you have. Include information about responsible positions you have held at school, such as being a member of the school council or a team captain. Include a short personal statement outlining your key qualities.

If you are invited for an interview, follow these simple rules for success:

- Dress appropriately and arrive on time.
- Shake hands firmly and look the interviewer in the eyes. Smile!
- Answer the questions with honesty. Share your good qualities and relevant experience.
- Always have a couple of questions prepared, to show how keen you are.
- Thank the interviewer for their time, and ask when you can expect to hear if you've been successful.

DiD YOU KNOW?

There are laws that govern the type of work young people can do and the number of hours they are permitted to work. Some countries also set minimum wages. Check the laws that apply to you before you take on a job.

FEEL-GOOD FACTOR

Find out what the Health and Safety guidance is for the job you do. Make sure you follow the rules, and never put yourself in any type of danger, no matter what an employer tells you to do.

Juggling a job

Taking on a job with regular shifts will make it easier for you to keep to your study plans. You will soon learn which parts of your life must change to make way for your new responsibility. If necessary, be prepared to give up, or cut down on, some of your leisure activities.

If your job has irregular working hours then you'll have to be ultra-organised. Put your timetable on the family notice board, so everyone in the family knows where you are going to be, and when. This will also help you become a reliable and punctual employee.

Whether you work in a shop or take on a paper round, be organised and professional about your work.

Time to move on

When you decide to leave a job it is polite – and sensible – to follow the proper protocol. You will be expected to give notice, which means giving your employer a reasonable time to replace you. A week's notice should be the minimum. Assuming you are leaving on good terms, you ought to ask your employer for a reference. It should give the dates you were employed, your position and a brief outline of your duties. It should also include positive comments about how well you performed these duties. This reference will help you find new work.

Impress in a job interview by dressing smartly and shaking hands.

Keeping track of your income and expenditure is a good practice to get into as soon as you start working.

Money matters

Oscar Wilde once said, 'When I was young I thought money was the most important thing in life; now I'm old I know that it is.' Many people would disagree that money is the most important thing in life, but there's no doubt that having some money is usually better than having none. Controlling your own income and expenditure is an important part of preparing for adulthood, so it helps to have some pointers to making the most of your money.

Credit cards let you buy things without having to pay immediately. With a debit card, the money comes out of your account straight away.

Balancing a budget

A budget is a money plan. It lists all the money you receive, and all the money you spend. A budget is also a planning tool, so you could use it to map the amount of income you expect to get, along with the amount you expect to spend. The difference between the two will be your profit – or loss. To avoid a loss, and therefore a debt, you have to balance your budget, by either finding alternative ways to make money or by coming up with ideas to cut back on your spending.

UNDERSTANDING MONEY

Money matters can be confusing, partly because of the vocabulary. Here are some useful money words:

Debt. This is money you owe to the bank, or someone else.

Income. This is money you receive, e.g. earnings and allowance/pocket money.

Inflation. This is the way the value of money tends to fall over time, so things cost more.

Interest. This is money paid to you in return for leaving your money in a savings account. You pay interest on a debt.

Overdraft. This is money the bank lends you; you'll usually be charged interest on an overdraft.

Tax. This is money people have to pay to the government when they have a job.

Mark Zuckerberg set up Facebook while he was still a teenager.

Making money

The simplest way to make money is ideal for the lazy; just put whatever you have into a savings account and leave it there. If the bank is able to offer you a good rate of interest, you will make some money. If the current rate of inflation is high, though, any extra money you make could be wiped out by higher prices. Nevertheless, saving money is a great habit to get into, and it means you'll always have an emergency fund when you need it.

Earning money is more difficult, of course. Most teenagers opt for jobs to supplement any allowance they receive, but a few show an extraordinary flair for innovation and business enterprise. Mark Zuckerberg, for example, was a 19-year-old college student when he launched Facebook. Now he's one of the world's richest men.

Saving money

Cutting back on what you spend can be tough, because it means doing without things you really want. Welcome to the world of adults! Work out which costs are essential, and which are more of a luxury – and you'll be able to see where you can start saving.

REAL LIFE

'I did a paper round for three years and saved enough money to buy all the gadgets I need to record and edit videos. I now post them on the Internet and make money from advertising revenue. I still do my paper round, because I'm saving for college.'
Josh (17)

Choices and Changes

You have many choices to make – about love, your social life, exams, work and a lot more – but you may still be struggling to work out who you are and what you want.

People who are naturally risk-takers are much more likely to threaten their health by experimenting with controlled drugs or alcohol than those who are more cautious by nature.

A roll of the dice

In the 1970s *The Dice Man*, a novel by Luke Rhinehart, was published and quickly became a cult classic. The story tells of a psychiatrist who wants to let the roll of a dice settle every decision for him. He is liberated from the agony of making choices but, without a moral framework helping him to weigh up the reasons for every choice, his life descends into tragedy and lawlessness.

The story illustrates how important good decision-making is, and shows that we all have to bear both moral and practical responsibility for the outcomes of our choices. Throwing a dice relies on luck, and is the coward's way; good decision-making takes wisdom and courage.

FEEL-GOOD FACTOR

Dopamine is a brain chemical that makes you feel good. Your body makes more dopamine when you take dangerous risks, like driving very fast. But it also produces dopamine when you try new things, take part in sport and challenge yourself in positive ways.

What's the risk?

One of the hardest things about making choices and decisions is that you have to take some risks; few outcomes are ever guaranteed. Better decisions are made when you have taken steps to minimise the risk of a bad outcome. That means:

- Taking time
- Weighing up the evidence
- Considering all possible outcomes.

Does that process sound typical of the teenagers you know? Of course not! One of the most exciting things about adolescence is that it is a time of excitement, spontaneity, innovation and risk-taking.

A LONGER LIFE

People who are risk-takers are 10 times more likely to take controlled drugs than people who are more naturally cautious. Young people are more likely to take risks, which partly explains why nearly half of new HIV/AIDS cases every year occur in people under 25.

In two minds

Risk may be about danger, but it is also about opportunity. Young people are usually more open to new ideas and experiences, but the flipside to this positive attribute is that you may be more prone to taking dangerous chances. No one knows why teenagers tend to take more risks than children or adults, but here are two possible reasons:

1. *During our evolution, it suited the human race to have young people who were risk-takers, who sought new environments and food sources for their families, and who were willing to confront danger.*

2. *Young people simply lack the wisdom and experience to be able to make sound judgements, but they will learn as they mature.*

One of the reasons you have parents, guardians and teachers is so you can benefit from their experiences. Listen to the advice they offer; you can choose not to follow it, but it makes sense to equip yourself with all the information you need to make good choices.

DiD YOU KNOW?

Most teenagers do not use drugs, most under-16s do not get drunk regularly, and most under-16s have never had sex.

Consider channelling your energy and desire for excitement into sports – bungee jumping or white-water rafting perhaps.

Choices and Changes

Everyone feels stressed out, worried or alone sometimes – it's perfectly normal.

All change

Adolescence is a time of enormous, all-consuming change. Like the transition from caterpillar to butterfly, you are undergoing a metamorphosis. There may be times when the physical, mental and spiritual changes you are experiencing become very painful and frightening. There may be other times when you feel as if you are a steady sailing boat, trying to carve its way through a sea of turmoil. It is worth remembering that your friends are likely to be dealing with changes, too. They can offer you advice, or they may benefit from your support.

Body blues

During puberty your body changes day by day. Teenagers often feel worried about these changes, and wonder whether they are 'normal'. The truth is, everyone starts and finishes puberty at a different time, and progresses through it in a different way. There is no 'normal' when it comes to

When you're a teenager, hormones can send your emotions all over the place, making you feel stressed.

bodies. However, feeling a little bit scared or insecure about these changes is normal. If you are feeling anxious about any aspect of how your body is changing, you can discuss it with your doctor in complete confidence.

Rocky waters

Everybody, young or old, is more likely to thrive and feel happy if their home life is settled and secure, and they feel loved. Sometimes those

REAL LIFE

'My best friend Paul starting acting all weird, ignoring me, not going out and stuff. So I dropped him. Turned out he was depressed because his dad was very ill. I felt bad because I didn't help him. We talk about it now, and I try to be there for him.'

Dan (14)

circumstances do not exist, though. Here are just some of the stressful situations you may have experienced or worry about:

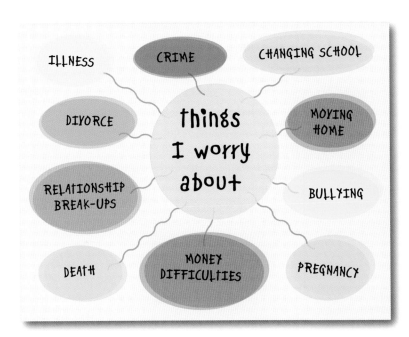

ILLNESS
CRIME
CHANGING SCHOOL
DIVORCE
things I worry about
MOVING HOME
RELATIONSHIP BREAK-UPS
BULLYING
DEATH
MONEY DIFFICULTIES
PREGNANCY

When we cannot control our environment and the changes that are being forced upon us, we feel very anxious. As you move towards adulthood you will be more affected by circumstances that your carers were once able to protect you from. Learning how to recognise the signs of anxiety and stress, and acquiring the skills to help you control them, will help you now and in the future.

The ups and downs of hormones

Hormones have a lot to answer for. During adolescence the sex hormones, oestrogen and testosterone, are not just causing lots of changes in your physical appearance; they are battling it out in your brain, too.

The levels of hormones in your blood are unstable, peaking and troughing in an unpredictable manner. This can cause swinging moods, higher levels of aggression and anger, and depression. On the plus side, these chemical messengers are one of the reasons you can fall in love and excel in sports. They will also help you develop an adult brain, capable of making considered judgements, planning a work schedule and – one day – caring for a family of your own.

FEEL-GOOD FACTOR

Try not to bottle up your feelings. When the prospect of change is making you feel anxious you will feel better if you talk about your concerns. Talking may help you identify what you most fear, and help you find practical solutions.

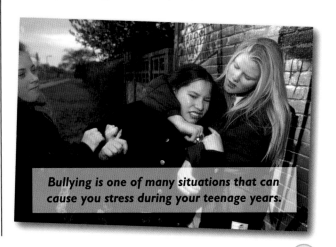

Bullying is one of many situations that can cause you stress during your teenage years.

Under Pressure

There are times in everyone's life when pressure builds up, and they feel very stressed. Recognising stress is the first step towards learning how to deal with it – and prevent it.

If you're under pressure it can affect your sleeping patterns and leave you awake and worrying throughout the night.

you to confront the danger, or flee from it (this is called the 'fight or flight' reaction). Your heart beats faster and stress hormones – adrenalin and cortisol – race around your bloodstream. You become more alert, focused, energetic and responsive to situations.

So stress can work positively to keep you from danger and help you perform better in challenging situations. Unfortunately, if you are stressed for a long time, it can have negative impacts, affecting your mental and physical well-being. Stress can:

• Make you feel more pain
• Give you digestive problems
• Damage your heart
• Reduce your immunity to illness
• Affect sleep
• Lead to depression.

What is stress?

Stress is your body's natural response to a bad situation. If your life is no longer balanced, you are feeling threatened, anxious or overwhelmed, your body may react with stress.

Stress is actually your body's way of protecting you from danger. When you are feeling threatened, your body tries to prepare

SYMPTOMS OF STRESS

Check out these signs to see if you might be suffering from the symptoms of stress:

• *Tiredness*
• *Crying*
• *Loss of appetite*
• *Sleeplessness*
• *Compulsive behaviour*
• *Feelings of alarm*
• *Use of drugs and alcohol.*

Why me?

Have you noticed how some people are able to remain very calm when others around them become agitated and tense? Everyone deals with stress differently, for a variety of reasons: genetics, the example set by our parents or siblings, environment and attitudes.

Scientists have found that males are more likely

to suffer poor health as a result of stress than females, and that adolescents who belong to a religious faith are often able to cope better with stress. This may be because they have more friends and strong social networks. Even caring for a pet can reduce your heart rate and blood pressure!

Life on the edge

Stress and anger-management issues are just two of a range of problems that many teens have to deal with. The flurry of emotions, physical changes, experiences at home and school, and hormonal instability – all associated with adolescence – can lead to an imbalance in mental health.

Teens who suffer this type of imbalance may develop problems such as phobias (irrational fears), eating disorders and obsessive-compulsive disorders (OCDs). The worst-affected young adults may resort to self-harm, become very depressed and even suicidal.

These are problems you cannot solve by yourself and they usually get worse if they are not treated. If you are suffering from any of these problems, it is important to find an adult you trust and feel comfortable with, so you can speak to them and get some help.

FEEL-GOOD FACTOR

Huge growth spurts in the brain are associated with extremes of emotion. It is no wonder that both toddlers and teenagers are prone to tears and tantrums! Unlike a toddler you can probably control yourself. Take a deep breath...

Combat pressure by taking a stress-busting class such as yoga or pilates, which focus on calming the mind and relaxing the body.

Dealing with stress

It is possible to deal with the negative effects of stress, and find ways to reduce or prevent it.

The first step is to identify which type of stress you suffer from:

1. *Rational. Some stress is brought about by rational factors – you don't have enough time to do your work, you have a large debt, you have upset a close friend. Rational stress can be tackled by having an organised, problem-solving attitude.*

REAL LIFE

'At exam time I feel as if I've got a squirming cat in my belly. Sometimes I get so nervous I am physically sick. It doesn't matter if my teachers tell me an exam isn't that important – it is to me.'

Li San (16)

2. *Irrational. Some stress is brought about by irrational fears – the house will burn down, my parents will die, no one likes me. Irrational stress is harder to deal with, because it may be brought about by low self-esteem, or an unrealistic understanding of situations. Counselling often helps people who are stressed for irrational reasons.*

Surfing the stress

How can you manage your stress?

1. *Prioritise it. Stress often comes from having too many things to do, or too many problems to deal with. Go back to page 12 and read the section on managing your time.*

2. *Solve it. Write a list of all the things that are making you feel anxious. Choose one problem, and identify a solution. Try and find a possible solution for all the problems on your list.*

3. *Cool it. Try to change your reaction to stressful situations. Practise slow breathing and relaxing your muscles. Try to turn anger into irritation, hate to dislike, etc.*

4. *Avoid it. If certain situations always make you stressed, see if you can avoid or change them.*

5. *Heal it. Stress is a physical reaction, so deal with the impact it's having on your body by looking after your health. Keep fit and well fed, take long walks, spend time with friends or pursuing your hobbies. Even stroking a cat or taking the dog for a walk can help reduce stress. Consider taking up stress-busting classes, such as art, yoga or meditation.*

Everyday stresses and pressures, such as school and exams, can take their toll if you don't learn how to deal with them.

Sports and hobbies are an important way of relieving pressure. It's important to make time for fun.

Keep your cool

Children and teenagers sometimes find it hard to control anger, and violent rages may result. Boys are more likely to have problems managing their anger than girls. Most doctors agree that anger is usually a symptom of another feeling, such as rejection, frustration or failure. If you get angry or violent, these suggestions may help you:

1. *Recognise the triggers that lead you to lose control, and take steps to avoid them.*

2. *Work out which things are valid reasons for getting angry (someone hits you), and those which are not (someone 'disrespecting' you).*

3. *Get organised. One of the main triggers for anger is poor time management. Is your life in balance?*

4. *Talk, talk and talk. It will help you find out why you are angry, and what you could do about it, in a more constructive way.*

FEEL-GOOD FACTOR

Sport and hobbies make a huge difference to how you cope with the stressful parts of your life. Make time for these activities, but don't use them to delay getting on with stuff that needs to be done. After one hour of gaming, that essay will still be waiting for you…

The Best You Can Be

A few years ago you probably knew exactly who you were and what you wanted. With adolescence, that changes. You are developing an adult 'sense of self'.

Magazines can give you the impression that you have to be model-thin to be attractive, but this isn't true.

What is self-esteem?

Self-esteem is a confidence in your abilities and worth. Teenagers often experience a drop in their self-esteem. It can be hard to get your head around who you are when your body, and your feelings, are constantly changing.

Young adults often feel a strong urge to belong to a group – to conform, or fit in. This pressure to feel accepted can make you even more conscious of your identity. The programmes you watch on TV, the magazines you read, and the way adults make you feel, can also affect your self-esteem.

DiD YOU KNOW?

Research has shown that adolescents who suffer from low self-esteem are more likely to take up smoking or have underage sex than those with more confidence.

You in the mix

People with low self-esteem may suffer a greater imbalance in their lives than their more confident peers. If you have a poor sense of your own value you may be reluctant to make friends, socialise in groups or get involved in sport. You might find it more frightening to seek out new experiences, or you may feel depressed. These are just some of the important reasons for improving your self-esteem. Boost your feelings of worth by following these suggestions:

1. *Cut out negative thoughts. It may sound simplistic, but it works. Every time a negative thought about yourself pops into your mind replace it with a positive one. Every day, write down at least three things you like about yourself.*

2. *Be realistic. Look around you – how many people are perfect in body and mind? No one is – our flaws make us human and unique.*

3. *Put a positive spin on it. Okay, so you made a mistake; treat it as an opportunity to learn, and don't make the same mistake again.*

4. *Get out there. Try out new things, take up a new hobby, set yourself goals and find time to help people who are worse off than you.*

Finding your own style is good – just make sure you're being true to yourself and not just following a trend so you 'fit in'.

Finding yourself

Young people who are trying to work out who they are demonstrate their inner turmoil in a variety of ways. You may recognise them:

- Status symbols – do you feel pressure to wear the 'right' clothes or trainers, own state-of-the-art technology, or flash your cash?
- Hero worship – while looking for a role in life, many teens aspire to be like certain celebrities or musicians.

FEEL-GOOD FACTOR

Write a list of 10 personal qualities that you admire and respect, such as honesty and humour. The list will help you identify the type of person you are, or want to be. Do your friends have some of these qualities? If not, what qualities do they have that you like?

- Rule-breaking – acts of rebellion show that you are separating from your parents or carers, while often pleasing your peers
- Acting older – engaging in activities that are associated with adults, such as smoking, drinking and sex, makes adolescents feel mature.
- Forming groups – belonging to a group can give you a powerful sense of belonging, social status and a group identity.

The Best You Can Be

Making connections

Communication is the way we pass information, to increase understanding. There are many parts of your brain that work together when you communicate. Neuroscientists have discovered that, because the brains of adolescents are developing and growing, there can be a change in the way teens are able to communicate. This can lead to misunderstandings, and even a breakdown in family relationships.

Blushing is a form of communication that we are unable to control, so it makes us feel very vulnerable. It tells people about possible emotions we may be experiencing.

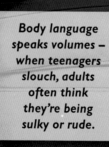

Body language speaks volumes – when teenagers slouch, adults often think they're being sulky or rude.

Body talk

Talking is one of the most obvious ways we can communicate, but we also use our body language to show how we are feeling. This is called non-verbal communication, and it is one area where teenagers often struggle; they may misread other people's body language, or give out misleading signals to those around them.

Teens with low self-esteem, for example, may hunch their shoulders and hide their eyes behind their hair. Adults often read this body language as sulkiness, rudeness or a lack of interest. On the other hand, children aged 11 to 12 lose their ability to read faces and understand other people's emotions. They don't recover this essential skill until they are in their late teens.

RED IN THE FACE

We blush when we feel strong emotions, such as anger, guilt and embarrassment. People who are shy or more anxious about other people's opinions of them blush most easily. Thankfully, it is something most of us grow out of as we become more confident.

Empathy – the emotion of understanding

Someone with empathy is able to share and understand someone else's feelings. Thanks to the way your brain is developing at the moment, it is quite likely that you do not score very highly on empathy skills.

In fact, scientists have found that the brains of teens and adults reacted differently when they were asked to deal with situations where empathy would help. It was found that adults used the bits of their brains that enabled them to imagine how their actions would affect other people's feelings. These bits of teen brains scarcely flickered into life!

The good news is that empathy does develop, and by the time you are an adult you will be much more sensitive to other people's feelings. In the meantime, try these tips:

• Ask – if you are not sure what someone is feeling, just ask them!
• Hear – listen to what people are telling you, and look at their body language at the same time.
• Imagine – how would you feel in the same situation?

Move like you mean it

When you are not feeling confident – at school, work or in a social situation – you can fool people into thinking you are. Think about what message your body language is giving out, and adapt it if necessary.

• Stand tall – you will gain height, and look more powerful. Holding your head high indicates self-esteem.
• Hands free – don't wrap your arms around your body; people will think you are unfriendly. Try not to touch your face, as this signals self-consciousness.
• Eye to eye – look people in the eye when you meet them, and hold their gaze when you talk, or listen, to them. This is one of the most powerful and engaging ways of communicating.

President Bill Clinton was a popular politician, who was known for his communication skills and ability to maintain eye contact.

The Best You Can Be

Uniquely you

How would you describe yourself? Are you outgoing, funny, attractive? Maybe you are intelligent, caring or shy? We all have an idea about what makes us unique – and the way we spend our time in work and play also helps to define us. So, you may also think of yourself as an academic, a football competitor, an animal-lover, a chess-player, a singer or an artist.

Hopefully, if you enjoy a well-balanced life, you will be able to think of a range of words to describe yourself. For some people, the list may be much shorter – perhaps limited to a single word or term, such as disabled, gay, dyslexic, autistic, carer, gifted and talented, foreign, orphan, bullied, elite athlete, bereaved, poor, ethnic minority, wealthy, homeless.

Made to a different mould

Sometimes the things that identify us are used to define us. They can become barriers to new experiences, friendships and activities. During the teen years, when there is pressure to fit in with a crowd, and a need to begin separating from the adults in your life, it can be particularly hard to be different. It doesn't matter whether the difference is one that you were born with, or one that has come about as a result of circumstance – it still hurts.

If the people around you have a one-dimensional view of your identity, abilities and attitudes, it can be exasperating trying to make them see the real you. Challenging people's preconceptions about you can become a lifetime's work.

DiD YOU KNOW?

Gay and lesbian young people are more likely to suffer depression, suicidal feelings and academic failure because of low self-esteem, caused by abuse, bullying and discrimination.

The most important thing, however, is that you keep challenging yourself to make the most of your strengths, and refuse to be defined by your differences or difficulties.

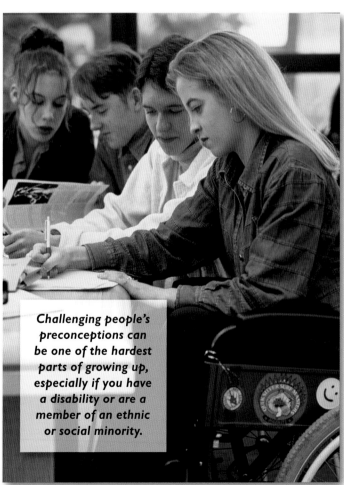

Challenging people's preconceptions can be one of the hardest parts of growing up, especially if you have a disability or are a member of an ethnic or social minority.

Get involved in projects that welcome people of all backgrounds and abilities – this will open you up to new experiences and new friends.

Finding a balance

Whatever your circumstances, you are entitled to enjoy a good education, a loving home life, the chance to exercise and relax, and to have opportunities to spend time with other young people. If you feel that you are being denied or deprived of these basic rights then it's time to ask for help. Parents or carers, teachers, school counsellors, social workers and organisations that work with young people are all obliged to ensure that every child and young person is able to both work and play in a safe and happy environment.

FEEL-GOOD FACTOR

Join groups or societies where you can meet other young people with similar interests, backgrounds or problems. You will find support, friendship and a sense of belonging that you may have been denied elsewhere.

CHILDREN'S RIGHTS

The United Nations Convention on the Rights of the Child 1990 states that no child should be discriminated against, and that all under-18s have a right to protection and development, and have the right to contribute towards decisions that affect them.

Friends and Family

As family bonds loosen you will find that people of the same age become some of the most important influences in your life. Balancing family and social relationships can be difficult, but there are ways of getting it right.

Friendships

Friends can help you deal with the demands of work, and to get the most from your downtime. They are easy to talk to, because they are probably going through the same changes and experiences.

For many teens, friendships matter more than almost anything else, which can cause imbalance in your life. Devoting all your time to your friends could mean that your studies suffer, or that you don't have time to concentrate on your other interests. Thanks to the Internet and mobile phones, you can now find out exactly what your friends are doing at any time – and they know everything about you.

Good friends, bad friends

Good friends offer you support, listen to your problems and respect you – but it is a two-way street. Being loyal, kind and attentive to your friends will help these relationships to grow, and to last.

Real friends are there to support you any time you need them. Know the difference between true friends and 'fairweather friends'.

Some friends fall short of the mark; they may expect you to drop everything so you can spend time with them. They may be kind one day, cruel the next. Fickle friends ignore you when someone 'better' comes along. You end up feeling used and lonely. People who try to force you to do things you don't want to do are not real friends. Choosing how to make good friends is a life skill. So is learning not to waste your time on the ones who keep hurting you.

Cyberbullying takes the form of picking on people through email or text messaging.

Groups and gangs

When you belong to a group of friends you feel secure, protected and accepted. Sometimes, however, a group begins to exert a cruel type of power. When this happens, it has transformed into a gang, and you should avoid it.

How to recognise a gang

• Gang members are expected to behave a certain way – there may be an unwritten set of 'rules' for all members.

FEEL-GOOD FACTOR

Beat the bullies by pretending that their taunts or actions don't affect you. Make it clear that you don't value their opinion anyway, and they may well leave you alone.

• Gangs are exclusive: members of a gang like to make themselves look, sound or behave differently to others.
• Gang members make themselves feel better by hurting people outside the gang. This is bullying.

Bullying

Bullying is behaviour that hurts other people. It includes name-calling, physical threats and attacks, stealing or damaging your belongings, spreading rumours and lies, and turning other people against you. Most people who bully have a low sense of self-esteem; they make themselves feel better by hurting others. Many people who bully have been bullied themselves.

Cyberbullying is relatively new. It involves bullying on the Internet – often on social-networking sites – sending insulting or intimidating texts, silent phone calls and nasty instant messages.

If you are a victim of any form of bullying you must seek help from an adult. Parents and teachers will support you, and the police have the technology to track down cyberbullies.

Adults grow up too

While you are carving a new path through life, the adults around you are trying to adjust to the new, ever-changing you. They know you are growing up and becoming independent, and are trying to help you in that process. As they let you go, the balance of their lives shifts dramatically.

For many parents or carers, this time can be traumatic, stressful and frightening. Since the day you were born they have had an enormous responsibility: looking after you. Don't be surprised that they still take that responsibility seriously and find this time of transition as difficult as you do.

Many teenagers feel like running away from home at some point, but there's always a better solution than life on the streets.

Bridging the divide

You may feel that a chasm is opening up between you and your parents, which will only get worse the more time you spend away from them. Maintaining good balance in your life includes being with your family. When you plan your week, consider setting aside time to be with your parents and siblings.

Trust and communication are two important parts of the teen-parent relationship. Your parents need to know that you can behave responsibly, are reliable, and that you are being honest with them. Keeping the lines of communication open will build trust; talking through problems or disagreements is more likely to get positive results than shouting and slamming doors. Here are some tips for earning brownie points with your parents:

- Volunteer information about where you are going and who you are seeing, before being asked.
- Ask them for advice; even if you don't take it, they'll be flattered.
- Empathise and show you care about their feelings.
- Do something helpful without being asked.
- Say something nice.

REAL LIFE

'I asked my kids to come on a family day out with me. They looked at me as if I was dirt, and refused to come. They have no idea how much I love them, and how much they hurt me sometimes.'
Matt (40)

What a chore!

One common reason that teens and their parents argue is the thorny topic of chores. It would be perfectly normal for you to put chores way down on your list of priorities – but if you want domestic harmony you should consider putting them rather higher!

Your parents want you to do your fair share of work around the house – and that's a reasonable expectation. They also want you to learn how to cook and clean, because when you leave home you will have to be able to do these things for yourself. There's no getting away from it, chores are dull, but they have to be done. Doing them without moaning is more likely to gain your parents' respect and rewards. Do extra chores, and you may be able to negotiate a bigger allowance or a later curfew.

Prove you can be trusted by helping out with younger brothers or sisters.

Helping out with chores around the house and garden will earn you brownie points and keep you fit, too.

Parent problems

As we grow up we realise that adults are not perfect – they can mess up too. Some adults, however, fall far short of what you have a right to expect from them. If poor parenting or abusive relationships of any type are harming you and your development then you should seek help. Speak to adults you can trust about these problems.

FEEL-GOOD FACTOR

Turn a 'no' into a 'maybe': instead of saying 'Can I do X?', ask 'Under what circumstances would I be allowed to do X?' It often works!

A Bright Future

Growing up is about so much more than the physical signs of change – it is about maturing, taking responsibility and making choices about your daily life, and your future.

Open doors

During your teens you are still a work in progress: many doors are open to you. You can learn new things, change your outlook and opinions – even your ability to understand and communicate complex issues improves with age.

In the past, your life has been organised by your parents and school; now that's changing and it's up to you where your journey takes you. Using tools that help you build balance in your life – and reach equilibrium – will help you emerge from adolescence with a healthy body and mind.

> ## REAL LIFE
>
> *'I loved being a teenager, but not all the time. Everything was either brilliant or absolutely terrible. I feel much more settled now. Those extremes were good, but only for a short while.'*
> Hannah (22)

Key skills for a balanced life

- Prioritising your life. Remind yourself of the important things that need to be done. Check that time for your studies, family, friends and leisure activities feature in your priorities.

- Planning a future. Working today is easier when you can imagine where it may lead. Think about what career you would like, and find out what you need to achieve to get there.

- Time management. Writing lists, plans and timetables can help you manage your time effectively – and get much more out of your

All the skills you're learning now are preparing you for your career and your whole life ahead. Enjoy it!

life. Set goals that you need to reach within a certain time.

- Avoiding distractions. Wasting time is easy, but it won't get you any nearer your goals. Remind yourself of your priorities, and exert some self-control.
- Discussing problems. Communication is the best way to start dealing with problems. If talking to your parents is hard, you could put your worries in a letter for them.
- Resting and relaxing. These parts of your life matter just as much as work. Finding time to relax or play is just as important as making time for studying.

Make it happen

Follow these five simple steps to stay on the path to success.

1. *Connect. Be sociable and spend time with other people, either working or playing. Ensure you keep eye contact with people when you talk to them. Keep the lines of communication open between yourself and your family.*

2. *Be active. Enjoy the fresh air, exercise your body and you will benefit both mentally and physically.*

3. *Enjoy. Stop and savour the special moments and the good times. Be aware of what is precious and good in your world, and take time to appreciate those many things.*

4. *Challenge. Remember that your developing brain craves learning and new, positive experiences so it can grow to its potential.*

5. *Give. Sharing and caring help us to gain a more realistic perspective of our own problems, and make us feel good. From giving a compliment, to giving your time, small acts of kindness are good for your inner self, and the people whose lives you touch.*

Becoming an adult means learning how to care and share. Get out there, challenge yourself, and perhaps help others in the process.

YOU'RE NOT ALONE

It is important to know that you are not alone; everyone goes through adolescence and many people will have experienced the difficulties or challenges that you are facing. Talking to friends, teachers and family can help, when help is needed. There are also organisations that can help you deal with specific problems or goals.

Glossary

adolescence the time of development between the beginning of puberty and adulthood.

anxiety a feeling of worry or tension.

blood pressure the force that blood exerts on the walls of the blood vessels. Blood pressure can vary according to age and general health.

body clock an internal time-keeper that controls some of your body's functions.

counselling a service that offers advice and support for people on a range of issues.

dehydration when the body does not have enough fluids in it.

depression an emotional state of gloom and deep sadness, or a medical condition characterised by the same emotions.

discrimination unfair treatment of a person, often because of their race, religion or sex.

empathy the power to imagine and understand someone else's feelings.

expenditure the amount of money you spend.

gene a section of DNA that carries a particular inherited characteristic, such as body shape.

genetics the study of genes and inheritance.

heart disease a narrowing or blockage of the blood vessels that provide oxygen-rich blood to the heart.

hormones chemical messengers produced by glands in the body. Hormones are transported by the blood to instruct cells and organs to work in a particular way.

irrational not logical, not following reason or good sense.

melatonin the hormone that brings on sleep.

menstruation when the lining of the uterus passes from the body as blood, known as a period.

metamorphosis a complete change of body form.

myelination the process of adding a myelin (fatty) layer to a neuron so it can transmit electrical impulses more quickly.

neuroscientist a scientist who studies the nervous system, especially the brain.

obesity when a person has an abnormally high amount of body fat.

oestrogen the female hormone that controls puberty and some parts of the reproductive system.

preconception having a belief about something before knowing the facts.

protocol an accepted code of behaviour.

psychiatrist a doctor who specialises in treating mental-health problems.

puberty the period during which adolescents reach sexual maturity and are capable of reproduction.

rational logical or reasonable.

sedative something that calms you down.

stress an emotional feeling of strain, tension or anxiety, and a physical state of the body.

supplements pills or liquids taken to add nutrients, such as vitamins, to the diet.

testosterone the sex hormone that controls some aspects of male puberty and the male reproductive system.

vitamin a substance that is essential, in very small amounts, for health.

yoga a belief system, and a type of exercise, that aims to bring peace and awareness through mental and physical exercises.